JON PAUL FIORENTINO

implosion
imprint

INSOMNIAC PRESS

Edited by Stephen Cain
Cover designed by Jon Paul Fiorentino
Cover art by Marc Ngui

Library and Archives Canada Cataloguing in Publication

Fiorentino, Jon Paul
 Asthmatica / Jon Paul Fiorentino.

ISBN 1-894663-86-1

 I. Title.

PS8561.I585A88 2005   C813'.6   C2005-900277-8

The publisher gratefully acknowledges the support of the Canada Council, the Ontario Arts
Council and the Department of Canadian Heritage through the Book Publishing Industry
Development Program.

Printed and bound in Canada

Insomniac Press
192 Spadina Avenue, Suite 403
Toronto, Ontario, Canada M5T 2C2
www.insomniacpress.com
www.jonpaulfiorentino.com

THE CANADA COUNCIL | LE CONSEIL DES ARTS
FOR THE ARTS | DU CANADA
SINCE 1957 | DEPUIS 1957

ONTARIO ARTS COUNCIL
CONSEIL DES ARTS DE L'ONTARIO

For Jamie

Contents

Foreword   9

I Wanna Be Your Alpha Male   13

Electrolux   21

Special Feature: Textual Commentary
       On *Electrolux* By The Author   35

Sarcasm Will Not Help Me Achieve My Goals   45

I'm Having A Seizure, What A Lovely Way
       To Say I'm Epileptic   55

Sissy Fists   65

Previously Enjoyed Crosswords   73

Milkman   81

Special Feature: *Milkman* (Deleted Scene)   93

Hail, Satan   97

Strapping Young Lads   107

Sicker Quicker   117

Rejected Essay Titles   125

Lookage   129

Insulin Chic   137

Asthmatica   143

The Longlist   147

FOREWORD

Hello, Dear Reader, and welcome to *Asthmatica*. I'm so glad you took the time to shoplift this book. But enough about you, this book is all about me, sort of. Every protagonist in *Asthmatica* is named Jonny. However, not all of the content of the book is true. For instance, while I may be an overweight, anxious, asthmatic, diabetic sissy, I would NEVER drink Coors Light. Most of these stories involve my family and I have used their real names as well (the character based on my brother, Jamie, is named Jamie; the characters based on my mom and dad are named Mom and Dad). It isn't fair to suggest that my family is anything like the characters of *Asthmatica*, but then again, life isn't fair, so they'll have to suck it up.

Speaking of sucking, you might remember me for my books of poetry, *Hello Serotonin, Resume Drowning* and *Transcona Fragments*. If you do, you might be thinking: *My God, JPF! You are such a talented poet and sexually attractive young man! Why stoop to write a book of comedic fiction?* This is a very good question. Thanks for asking, Mom. The answer is simple: I don't care what you think. The truth is, I have always loved the genre of the short story — in the same way a grown man might love a fairly adjudicated beard-growing or glue-sniffing contest. In many ways, *Asthmatica* is a book about love, memory and family values. Our heroes, all named Jonny, find themselves in situations typical to the genre of short fiction: making love to a vacuum cleaner, fantasizing about being strapped with a provincially approved strap, learning to drive drunk and getting to know Satan. It's salt of the earth type stuff and I'm just the type of author to document it — a complete hack. Also, you will find various little comedy bits that were originally written for *Matrix* magazine. These bits generally take aim at the often too conservative world of Canadian Literature. If you happen to be a member of this world and feel that you are being made fun of, please know this: I am an avid reader and ardent lover of Canadian Literature. So, in these comedy bits, I am really making fun of myself, but perhaps more importantly, I am also really, really making fun of you.

Well, the magical world of *Asthmatica* awaits you, Dear Reader, and I shouldn't hold you up for much longer. It is important for me to point out a couple of critical things before I let you go. First, my family and friends have been tremendously supportive and really have embraced the crucial difference between autobiography and fiction. And second, I was breastfed until I was eighteen — this may seem a little too long, but I think the results speak for themselves.

JPF
DECEMBER 11, 2004
MONTREAL, QC

I WANNA BE YOUR ALPHA MALE

My parents sucked. They used to make me mow the lawn despite my lethal allergy to freshly cut grass. On a weekly basis, they made me wear a surgical mask, start up the old gas engine mower and mow the fucking lawn. There I was, wearing a baby-blue surgical mask, pushing this obnoxiously loud John Deere mow-machine over our lush, green grass. As one might imagine, the neighbourhood kids were ruthless. They called me everything from fuckface, to sissy, to douchebag, to Dr. Lawnmower. Dr. Lawnmower. I liked that. It sounded kinda cool — like a supervillain. When I was finished mowing the lawn, I had to empty the bag of grass clippings. My entire body was one huge, blazing rash except for an oval-shaped patch of white skin on my face where the mask had been; and, because of my asthma, I generally had to take a triple-dose of inhaled steroids and ventolin to catch my breath. I am not bitter.

Once, when I was around fourteen, after emptying the grass-clippings into an orange garbage bag, I heard a taunt ringing in my ear: "Hey Dr. Lawnmower! You're stupid, you stupid lawn-mowing fuckface!" There was a group of four boys on the street, much younger than me, pointing and laughing at me. "Dr. Lawnmower! Dr. Lawnmower! Fuckface! Douchebag!" I ripped my mask off and charged toward the kids like a raging, asthmatic bull. I inspired no fear. As I approached the clear leader of the taunting band, I began to swing my fists wildly. The combination of physical activity and allergenic activity resulted in a blackout before I could land one effeminate punch. I lay there, my body on the edge of the grass, my head on the curb. My parents told me later that when they arrived on the scene, the boys were laying the boots to me. I think my brother, Jamie, may have done a little stomping himself as my parents called the ambulance — that would have been just like him.

Anyway, before my eyes opened in the St. Boniface Hospital emergency room to a fluorescence of antiseptic, anesthetized, swirling hospital-type stuff, I saw you in my dreams. Bright orange hair, wild, untamed freckles, a gap between your two front teeth just like David Letterman. You were my dream girl — similar to Anne of Green Gables but without the Green Gables and much hotter, and willing do to really freaky things that Anne of Green Gables would never do unless she was paid a shitload of money or she was addicted to heroin. Even as repeated injections of Prednisone were yanking me from my unconscious state, the vision of you remained clear. You were, and are, with me.

My brother tried to convince me that I would never marry. He told me I was too fat and asthmatic for marriage. He always told me that the most I could hope for was to be a general labourer who pays for sex on a monthly basis and has a disturbingly large collection of fetish pornography. He even had a nickname for me: Future Blue-Collar Pervert. Actually, he had a few nicknames for me including: Big Wheezy Sweat Monkey and Captain Failure. General labourer, fetishist — I couldn't quite make it. I had to settle for a career in literature. And I'm not happy about it. I know you can make things better. I know you are waiting for me somewhere.

Now that I'm all grown up and my parents have been safely dis-patched to a retirement community in Sarnia and my brother has moved to New York to pursue his dream of becoming the best white Latino rap artist since Gerardo, that dude who sang "Rico Suave," I feel a sense of freedom I have never felt before. I want to pursue my dreams too. I want a girl like you. In fact, I want you. A girl with taste and style and a house. I bet you have your very own house. I want to turn that house into a home. I want to have fat asthmatic babies with you. How much do you pay on your mortgage each month? $700? $800? I know I can afford my share. Let me win your bread. Let me pay some affable, pimple-faced kid with no allergies to mow our lawn. Let's watch him from the window; I will hold you close and we will watch him manicure our lush grass in perfectly symmetrical rows. You might have the heart to offer him lemonade or, if we are feeling perfectly subversive, a cold Coors Light, or per-haps some homemade wine. Perhaps we can share the hobby of making homemade wine. The first attempts might be a little cloudy but we'll get the hang of it. With you by my side there would be nothing I couldn't do. Except maybe sit-ups. Those are really hard. Maybe I will videotape our lovemaking and we can go over it as if it was game film. (I will wear a surgical mask.) You can be my coach. No. I will be the coach. You will be my star player. Hey. Listen. Screw that. I want to mow your lawn. Screw that hypothetical kid. He can get a hypothetical paper route. Let me mow your lawn. I wanna mow your lawn. It will be worth the rash, the hives, the lack of oxygen. I wanna mow your lawn. I wanna be your alpha male.

ELECTROLUX

The mirror stage is a drama whose internal thrust
is precipitated from insufficiency to anticipation.
— Jacques Lacan

My heart tapped me on the shoulder and whispered
in my ear: "Don't be a pussy all your life."
— Smoking Popes

My sexual awakening from latency was encased in a world of hyper-suburbia: the artificial lakes, the endless, tasteless landscaping, the stuccoed homes, the claustrophobic playgrounds with sparkling swingsets and plastic slides. My home was immaculate — a two-storey temple to the nuclear family. My room was above the garage; my reading light would illuminate my window into the early morning, my consciousness slowly developing under the guidance of texts such as the 1985 *NHL Yearbook* or Althusser's "Ideology and Ideological State Apparatuses (Notes towards an Investigation)." My room was always perfectly clean. I vacuumed daily.

Mom taught me to vacuum when I was a toddler. She commanded the Electrolux, negotiating tricky spaces between the back of the couch and the wall, and I was right behind her, right behind her floral print dress, with my Fisher-Price Corn Popper push toy, the multi-coloured balls popping upward and impacting against its plastic, translucent dome. I would cover every stretch of carpet that she did. As she ended her rounds, she would save a spot of dirty carpet for me and hand over the real thing. The vacuum wand shook in my tiny hands and Mom would stand behind me and guide me over the dirt, leaving immaculate shag and satisfying me.

I came for the first time in my spacious walk-in closet. I came without much stroking; it was more of a staring contest between me and my penis. I was eleven years old, almost twelve, hovering between sexual ambiguity and bliss. Sexuality had a strong grip on me despite my participation in the latent stage; and, because of my readiness for the realm of the ejaculatory, I quickly moved from anticipatory coming to becoming. I became a complete sexual entity from that point on — intricately detached from the image of the shy, pubescent eleven-year-old huddled in the corner of my closet, infinitely aroused by Revlon advertisements in my mom's *Good Housekeeping* magazines.

After the first decade of living, one is thrust into the most volatile social context widely known as Junior High. In this tragic realm there is a cruel lack of distinction between a child and a teenager. It seemed to me that my grade six schoolmates had all bridged this gap while I was hovering — continuously hovering. The truth is, we were all hovering — there were not any worse incarnations of puberty surrounding me; it was simply that I couldn't perceive things in this relative way at the time. I judged purely on the aesthetic aspects of my peers. I was a shy and fey boy, desperately trying to anchor myself down in hockey statistics. For extended periods, I would abandon my fascination with semiotic theory and Freudian discourse. I would attempt to commit manhood to memory: "What a goddamned pussy! Why didn't he hit him? Drop the gloves! Drop the gloves!" Dad, immovable on the couch beside me, would begin to glow with pride at the sound of such utterances; my male friends would join in a chorus of these taunts; my mom would sigh and make a passing comment about violence in sports.

It was true that I did have a mild sports fetish. But my most intense fetishism was found in the realm of the socially inappropriate. Mom's sequined and lamé blouses still fit loosely on my delicate-yet-big-boned frame. And after school, in the hours of sweet latchkey silence, I would writhe to the melodious strains of Abba's *Supertrooper*, covered in the loudest, tackiest glitter on my parents' expansive queen-size bed. My cross-dressing allowed me to feel like an aesthetic object — self-contained, beautiful. All possibilities were open until I heard the creak of the door opening and my parents' voices filling the alabaster temple, the sickly mausoleum that was our home.

Out of the vortex of pre-pubescence, at age thirteen, I took a lover. My lover had lived in my house longer than I had — a part of the family really. It was fiendishly inappropriate and this must have been the lure. One night, when my parents had departed for a deca- dent evening at The Velvet Glove Dinner Theatre, I was in a dream- like state, sampling my parents' whiskey under the backdrop of the Jets vs. North Stars game which flickered like abstract candlelight; my eyes met with the creamy beige contours of the Electrolux Golden J vacuum cleaner. I was drawn in by its Freudian lure — its emblematic femininity and masculinity, pure sexuality was before my very eyes. It was a canister model with smooth, pleasing con- tours. It featured a telescopic wand and more importantly, a detach- able hose — a silky, snaky, winding figure — a phallic emblem granted, but also a portal. It felt soft against my hands, my lips, my tongue, my skin. It was a perfect fit. Our trysts were discrete, yet passion-filled, as we merged in pubescent wails of delight and veiled shame. The Electrolux would desperately squeal for more air and I would squeal in harmony. It would bring me to the most urgent growth spurts, sucking me into its being. I could always see my reflection in the chrome of the floor attachment. Mirror stage. My lover. It was tireless, calling me endlessly from the storage closet, or sprawled out on the living room floor after being put to work. To this day I can hear its sexy, wheezy voice: "Jonny ... Jonny? Where are you Jonny?"

"I'm coming."

The Electrolux used to leave the most beautiful love marks on me — the most symmetrical hickeys possible. I read them as symbols: circles of perfection. My first experience with vacuum bliss was short lived, as Dad walked in on us one frigid November afternoon when I should have been at school and he had left work early. The look on his face was unforgettable — an intense expression of merged disappointment and abject fear. He had never asked for this — this level of parenting that transcends the mundane interpella-tions of "You! Clean up your room!" or "If you don't eat your veg-etables, you can't have any dessert!" The discipline was swift and inappropriate as it left me with brutal marks that, although the lash-es from his monogrammed belt were able to straddle the line between deterrent pain and absolute sadistic bliss, seemed inevitably parental and cruel. In the middle of Dad's waist, rested a large gold-plated D. When the belt came off, and I began to cower, it most def-initely stood for Dad. When juxtaposed with the perfection of my vacuum hickeys, his iconographic marks of punishment were sim-ply wrong: the purple letter D never fully rendered and always in erasure. Often the Electrolux would witness these moments between Dad and me. It would sag guiltily in the corner of the room or stand upright against the wall as if it were about to jump to my defense. When I visit Mom and Dad at the old place, I sneak away to the storage closet and I gaze in the direction of that old Electrolux. I am consistently puzzled as to why they never got rid of it; but I am equally pleased with the fact that there will always be a part of me left behind in that vacuum cleaner.

At thirteen, I had one close friend. His name was Kyle and his face was angelic: replete with the most dreamy combination of freckles and pimples that blended into unique ambiguity. He was a good friend. His house was filled with the most glorious pornography, subtly hidden under mattresses and in the back of closets like Easter eggs. My home, on the other hand, was a museum of repression and cleanliness. Kyle would have me over for the night on occasion; and, when Mrs. Anderson had tucked us in nice and tight, tracing both of our bodies with a motherly hand, and all the lights in the house went out, and Mr. Anderson's symphonic snoring enveloped the place like the comforting sound of an old furnace, our night would begin. We would stealthily pillage the house, finding stacks of *Penthouse* magazine and BETA video tapes entitled *Adventures in Humping* or *Indiana Bones and the Temple of Hump*. I was drawn into Kyle's video world of mimetic sexual representation — gloriously effected fake orgasms emoted under the sounds of synthetic funk. We would sit still, amid the seductive moans of some old 1980s porn diva. We engaged in simultaneous masturbation. At times, our eyes would lock and we would connect on some kind of psychic plane. In the warm, sticky indeterminacy of these moments, Kyle was my angel. He kept watch over me and encouraged me to stroke my way to sexual epiphany. Kyle's face was alive with a healthy blush that swallowed his freckles. I think of these experiences with a strange combination of nostalgia and shame. This shame is based simply in the fact that all we really wanted from each other was relief — in this sense we were using each other. Although, I suppose that's what friends do. Kyle would always wait for me to come first. I was relieved. It felt right.

Visits to Kyle's place always seemed to ground me in a kind of linear sexual state and I would remain there for weeks at a time. (That is to say, the retrievable memories of both *Adventures in Humping* and the orgasmic purple glow of Kyle's face would linger.) But as inevitable as getting an erection during the bus ride home, I would return to less conventional means of sexual expression. While I witnessed every pimply-faced peer take a weekly girlfriend, I seemed static in my solitary sexuality. Kyle was spending hours every day with his tongue down Tina Black's throat. I would walk by him slowly after school and he would always be sucking face with his eyes wide open. My mirror image had shattered. Every once in a while he would lift his freckled hand from Tina Black's back pocket to acknowledge me with a polite wave. His lips did not detach from hers for the rest of that school year; I retreated into that walk-in closet, developing my imaginative and regenerative memory to the point of unspeakable sophistication.

I came out of the closet to play ball hockey with other pubescent rejects. My elitist, beauty myth-biased attitude toward such people seemed now to be a function of social conditioning, and this attitude dissolved like any childish notion should. We were an amalgam of baby fat and crooked teeth. There were braces and retainers and mountainous blackheads swirling in the most intense, violent sessions of ball hockey ever played. My sexual sensibility was once again captured in notions of marking the body. This time, vicious stick work was my vehicle for sexual gratification. I slashed and butt-ended anyone and everyone. I would get into the most fabulous fistfights — dropping my garbage mitts and hurling my fluxing body onto another adolescent, and we would roll around in the freshly plowed street tasting salt and each other's fists. The sexual excitement would build to a feverish peak later in my room as, in silence, I placed my stick in the corner of the closet, caressed its taped-over butt end and slid into the incandescent realm of fantasy. I would project a more angelic visage onto the tactile memory of the androgynous pudge of my latest hockey rival, desperately flipping through Mom's *Good Housekeeping* in order to find the perfect face to transpose: perfect! A maternal figure suggestively gripping the newest model of the (clearly inferior) Hoover vacuum cleaner! At the same time I was longing for Kyle's archival stash of fully realized sexual performance. Real pornography is economical and I had decided that this is both its functionality and its charm; and, of course, absence makes the heart grow fonder.

There was a time before that first, unexpected rush of semen in my walk-in closet, where it seemed I was most suited to develop and foster relationships with girls exclusively. Girls seemed delicate and angelic — just like I thought myself to be. My perfect angel would resemble a *Good Housekeeping* woman, modelling some household appliance with a secure permasmile, encouraging me to be the best that I could be; and everything I would do would be for her. Then Kyle confused things for a while — my sexuality became more complex as I began to see Kyle as angelic and worthy of affection. I had considered Kyle a social anomaly. However, puberty performed a sickly, abortive act on my formative friendships. Kyle willed himself to grow two feet in a matter of months and elevated himself to the status of local legend — often banging three or more girls at house parties I had no hope of ever going to. The girls I had previously befriended began to seek out the awkward differences exhibited by the most typically masculine of the boys; and I was simply too close to being a girl myself. I became an isolated young man, with either sex on either side of me. And I was looking to perform some kind of inaccessible diplomatic act by cross-dressing my way to a new realization of sex or gender. Of course, all of this was done in the privacy of my antiseptic home. I was wholly alive when a sparkled blouse began to chafe, at the climax of "Moon River" when I would mouth the words "it's just around the bend" and writhe in the most performative state.

At the lowest point of pubescence, punctuated with various fetishes toward office supplies and action figures, something peculiar happened. Girls became angelic again. (Not just the ones in *Good Housekeeping*, but real ones — real live breathing bipeds.) I was fifteen and curiously emerging as an average-looking individual. This granted me access to the most transient social networks and an unspoken pass to school dances and house parties. I was fully awakened to real possibilities by Stacy Bellinger — she was a sight at five feet, seven inches with her tightly crimped blond hair, tight acid-washed jeans and even tighter Motley Crüe T-shirt which served to accent her emerging breasts — everything about her was tight. During regular school hours, I was a target for her aggression. I was ritualistically kicked in the groin by this powerful cloakroom diva. And, in retrospect, I enjoyed every kick despite the immediacy of pain and the paralysis as I lay in bliss, doubled over, under the shadow of my locker. But on certain nights, during school dances, I became her dance partner. And with my height of just over five feet

I was in heaven. I would lay my head on her breasts and escape into a fantastical world in which I would lay down with Stacy in a pastoral setting with women from the pages of *Good Housekeeping* dancing topless in the green fields of spring.

The most repellent, yet fascinating, teenage boys wearing their AAA Hockey jackets let me know that it was important to get laid early and often. Getting laid could mend the fracture between socially acceptable masculinity and myself. I wanted to get laid. Stacy's breasts were symbols of freedom, like hubcaps on a Chevette glistening with a fresh coat of Armor-All. They haunted me throughout my ninth grade until I finally broke down and asked her breasts, in a triumphant moment, to the movies. After I regained my breath and I looked up to her from my usual fetal position under my locker, she bent down beside me, my testicles still sending out sharp pangs of brilliant pain, and she whispered a seductive "Yes." My gaze ascended to her dark green eyes. Her face was mildly flush. My face was a volcanic terrain, sweat shooting out of pores, veins threatening to burst.

It was a wet, warm spring evening when I met her at the bus stop. She was not wearing her usual non-conformist uniform but a floral-print dress instead; her hair was set with two identical butterfly barrettes. We said nothing as the bus rumbled onward to the mall. I was so distracted by my anxiety and the juxtaposition of our bodies, which suggested that perhaps she was one of those good babysitters, taking the kid out for the evening, that I did not even get a hard-on from the bus ride. I bought our tickets and we sat through all eighty-seven minutes of some banal teen comedy: *Humping Academy* or something. To tell you the truth, I was completely fixated by the silhouetted figure beside me. Spring had set in and so had my manhood, my maturity. I was about to arrive.

In mutual silence, we decided to walk home through the damp, expansive, underdeveloped fields of Transcona. I elevated my hand until it touched hers and she took it in with authority. We stopped behind the Oxford Heights Community Club and in between the unkempt, thawed-out, hockey rinks, under the supervision of dull amber light we exchanged awkward, comical kisses — she, like a hunchback, and me, like a tragic child on the tip of his toes, trying to reach the water fountain. She tasted like the perfect mixture of salt and vinegar chips and watermelon gum. Her tongue was insistent. I took comfort in the swelling sexuality of the moment and the fact that she seemed quite assertive about everything. Despite the damp chill that had settled in, she slipped out of her dress and carelessly let it drop into a puddle. I wanted to reach out and grab her but she didn't have a handle. I didn't know where to grab. She took my hand and guided it over her breasts, and with unspoken instruction my hand danced across her pale body. I could feel her shivering, but I had no words: I couldn't ask her if she was too cold. This was Stacy Bellinger; she was in charge.

She pulled me into the visitor's bench and she stretched out along the flaking paint and splintered wood. This place was an absolute mess. It could use a thorough going-over. As she slowly inched her way out of her underwear, I reached an unexpected level of stillness and fear. I was in the slot, uncovered, in front of a wide open net. And then without a word I left her. Paralyzed by the reality of the situation, the frighteningly non-representational reality, I left her there. I ran like a fumbling schoolboy toward the street with the chill of the premature spring night enveloping my body. My untied boots pounded their way to freedom. I trampled blades of grass that had emerged despite the muck and sand of the field. The world was sick and pale and flat. No matter how fast I ran, I remained visible — a sad pubescent figure, legs pumping in tragicomic fast-forward. There was no horizon, just a damp field that lay dormant like endless carpeting. A single word echoed from the seemingly unoccupied hockey rink behind me. Stacy's shrill angelic voice carrying through the still evening air:

"Pussy."

I slid into my house to find it unoccupied, with an explanatory note on the fridge. I made my way up to my parents room and slid into Mom's gold lamé blouse and Dad's Winnipeg Jets sweat pants. I made my way to the living room and sprawled out on the couch, momentarily losing myself in the television — images of grown men whipping around a hockey puck and crashing into each other with inexplicable aggression. Across the ceiling, the wintery light from the television revealed the brooding shadow of an Electrolux Golden J vacuum cleaner which had been propped up against the coffee table, in haste.

SPECIAL FEATURE: TEXTUAL COMMENTARY ON *ELECTROLUX* BY THE AUTHOR

The Epigraphs

> *The mirror stage is a drama whose internal thrust*
> *is precipitated from insufficiency to anticipation.*
> — *Jacques Lacan*

> *My heart tapped me on the shoulder and whispered*
> *in my ear: "Don't be a pussy all your life."*
> — *Smoking Popes*

As an author, it is important to choose your epigraphs wisely. The Jacques Lacan epigraph is clearly a strategic ploy to seduce the reader into believing I have read Jacques Lacan. Of course I haven't. Who do you think I am? J. Hillis Miller? That shit is hard to read and it gives me a headache. Having said that, I think it is important to have a good working knowledge of Critical Theory and, specifically, Lacanian theories of psychoanalysis and self.

In harsh and effective juxtaposition lies the other epigraph from the obscure Sissy Rock band Smoking Popes. They are best known for supporting Morrissey on his 1999 North American tour and for their lead singer's unfortunate conversion to Christianity. The band split up shortly after Josh Caterer, the aforementioned lead singer, began talking incessantly about Jesus in the year 2000. No doubt, the conversion of this talented singer/songwriter was related to Y2K anxiety and paranoia. He is, truly, the Cat Stevens of our generation. This epigraph reveals my ongoing allegiance with the principles and practices of "pussydom."

The First Paragraph

My sexual awakening from what we call latency was encased in a world of hypersuburbia: the artificial lakes, the endless and tasteless landscaping, the stuccoed homes, the claustrophobic playgrounds with sparkling swingsets and plastic slides. My home was immaculate — a two-storey temple to the nuclear family. My room was above the garage; my reading light would illuminate my window into the early morning, my consciousness slowly developing under the guidance of texts such as the 1985 NHL Yearbook *or Althusser's "Ideology and Ideological State Apparatuses (Notes towards an Investigation)." My room was always perfectly clean. I vacuumed daily.*

I enjoyed writing this first paragraph very much. There were some linguistic choices that I was forced to make from the outset: "hypersuburbia" is my neologism. It is important to establish authorial authority in the opening sentences of one's story. I believe the establishment of this term gives me the authority to say "Hey! I'm the author here! I made up a new word! Check it out! It's pretty super awesome!" I like that. I have a penchant for the dash and — perhaps I am being self-indulgent here — it really illustrates to the reader that the author cares about punctuation. I like to go for the gusto. The last sentence reveals a curious economy amid a text that is very adjectival and excessive: "I vacuumed daily." I like that. I think it says so much about vacuuming and chronology.

Stacy

I was fully awakened to real possibilities by Stacy Bellinger — she was a sight at five feet, seven inches with her tightly crimped blond hair, tight acid-washed jeans and even tighter Motley Crüe T-shirt which served to accent her emerging breasts — everything about her was tight. During regular school hours, I was her target for aggression. I was ritualistically kicked in the groin by this powerful cloakroom diva. And in retrospect, I enjoyed every kick despite the immediacy of pain and the paralysis as I lay in bliss, doubled over, under the shadow of my locker. But on certain nights, during school dances, I became her dance partner. And with my height of just over five feet I was in heaven. I would lay my head on her breasts and escape into a fantastical world in which I would lay down with Stacy in a pastoral setting with women from the pages of Good Housekeeping *dancing topless in the green fields of spring.*

Stacy is really a composite character; she is every teenage boy's pleasure and bliss in the Barthesian sense of those terms. There is a problematic male gaze operating here. Stacy is perhaps too much image and object and too little character. I am personally offended by my own inability to provide her with the complex text she deserves. Therefore, please enjoy the following list of innovative gender theory texts.

Bornstein, Kate. *Gender Outlaw*. New York: Routledge, 1994.
Butler, Judith. *Gender Trouble*. New York: Routledge, 1992.
Foucault, Michel. *The History of Sexuality*. New York:
Pantheon, 1978.
Stein, Gertrude. *Tender Buttons*. New York: Claire-Marie, 1914

Vacuum Love

... the Electrolux Golden J vacuum cleaner. I was drawn in by its Freudian lure — its emblematic femininity and masculinity, pure sexuality was before my very eyes. It was a canister model with smooth, pleasing contours. It featured a telescopic wand and more importantly, a detachable hose — a silky, snaky, winding figure — a phallic emblem granted, but also a portal. It felt soft against my hands, my lips, my tongue, my skin. It was a perfect fit. Our trysts were discrete, yet passion-filled, as we merged in pubescent wails of delight and veiled shame. The Electrolux would desperately squeal for more air and I would squeal in harmony. It would bring me to the most urgent growth spurts, sucking me into its being. I could always see my reflection in the chrome of the floor attachment. Mirror stage. My lover. It was tireless, calling me endlessly from the storage closet, or sprawled out on the living room floor after being put to work. To this day I can hear its sexy, wheezy voice: "Jonny ... Jonny? Where are you Jonny?"

"I'm coming."

This is a special part of the story for me. Jonny is named for the first time and this is during a recollection of vacuum sex. This presents the reader with a very psychologically sophisticated understanding of "self." Part of this story is very autobiographical. As a child I did sample whiskey from my parents' cabinet and I most certainly watched my share of Winnipeg Jets games. The inclusion of the Winnipeg Jets in this text was essential for me. The legacy of failure coupled with the team's demise and move to Phoenix connotes something very important about loss, latency, and dormancy. As for the vacuum, I wanted to make the vacuum a clear metaphor for the bisexuality in all of us. I think that is clear. However, I need to make one thing very clear. This story is not completely autobiographical: I have never, as a child or an adult, had sex with an Electrolux. This is exclusively the character Jonny's experience. The author, Jon Paul Fiorentino, has always been more of a Hoover man.

Daddy

The discipline was swift and inappropriate as it left me with brutal marks that, although the lashes from his monogrammed belt were able to straddle the line between deterrent pain and absolute sadistic bliss, seemed inevitably parental and cruel. In the middle of Dad's waist, rested a large gold-plated D. When the belt came off, and I began to cower, it most definitely stood for Dad. When juxtaposed with the perfection of my vacuum hickeys, his iconographic marks of punishment were simply wrong: the purple letter D never fully rendered and always in erasure. Often the Electrolux would witness these moments between Dad and me. It would sag guiltily in the corner of the room or stand upright against the wall as if it were about to jump to my defense. When I visit Mom and Dad at the old place, I sneak away to the storage closet and I gaze in the direction of that old Electrolux. I am consistently puzzled as to why they never got rid of it; but I am equally pleased with the fact that there will always be a part of me left behind in that vacuum cleaner.

D is for Daddy. I think that this section, which explores the line of demarcation between the vacuum and the father, is quite sad. Thankfully, it ends with a delightful double entendre: "there will always be a part of me left behind in that vacuum cleaner." I think it is fair to say that this is my version of "Daddy." Although my version is contained in a section of a comedic short story and is much more poignant than Plath's old poem. The notion of interpellation is important here. It might be a good idea to highlight that word with a highlighter, or perhaps circle it. If I was to choose a Hollywood actor to portray the part of the father, I think I would choose Elliot Gould. Not so much because I think he could pull it off, but I think he needs the work. If I could choose a Hollywood actor to play the vacuum, it would be a toss-up between Anne Heche and Brian Dennehy. For more information on Brian Dennehy, visit your local library or consult the following webpage:

<http://www.mindspring.com/~billandsue/briandennehy.html>

ASTHMATICA

PRO
SET

Liquidation

Hypermart
Liquidation Baby

SARCASM WILL NOT HELP ME ACHIEVE MY GOALS

Mr. Hardman looked across at me with a tinge of fear in his eyes. He needed help firing me; this is why Mr. Linville sat beside him. Mr. Linville simply looked bored. I had worked at Hypermart for two years and a bit. Within the first week, I had dyed my hair blue; it matched the colour of the sharp-looking smocks that we all had to wear. Mr. Hardman put me on probation for that. Prick. I thought probation was just a figure of speech but it turned out that it actually meant something. They start watching you with the security cameras, and if you spend more than five minutes on the phone, you generally get busted and that goes into the probation file.

I was shuffled between the hardware, menswear, and sporting departments, and eventually I ended up as a cashier. To me, this was the sweetest plum of the Hypermart experience. It meant that I could happily assess every sad, wretched customer's purchases and let them have it in my own, subtle way: "Excellent choice, ma'am. The econo 50-pak of Hypermart Brand disposable douches is the pinnacle of both quality and value. Disposable douches, now that's an innovation, eh, ma'am? I don't wanna see a douche that isn't disposable. The future is now! Am I right, ma'am? Ma'am? Well, let's see what else we got here ..."

So, anyway, they sat there, these two mounds of bureaucratic muscle — tight neckties, Hypermart classic menswear dress shirts, wedding rings, every emblem that signified success.

Hardman spoke first. "So Jonny, do you have any idea why we've asked you in here?"

"You finally gathered up the courage to ask for a threesome?"

Linville yelped, "Hey! Watch it mister. You know, that's always been your main problem. Your sarcasm. Sarcasm will not help you achieve your goals."

I rolled my eyes. "Hey that's really sage advice sir. Thanks a bunch." But I did take a mental note. Sarcasm will not help me achieve my goals. Hardman whipped out his thick, thick file.

Hypermart ™ "Where quality is king"
677 Regent Avenue West, Winnipeg, MB R4F 6F4

Incident Report. Employee: Jonny. Status: PROBATION
December 11, 2001

After being warned about not tucking in his shirt, Jonny apologized and acted like he understood. I explained the importance of being a team player and looking like a Hypermart family member. Jonny said that he appreciated the family and team metaphors and said that he had never thought of it that way. Around ten minutes later, Jonny made the following announcement on the store intercom:

"Attention Hypermart shoppers, as you know, Hypermart values family and teamwork above all else. That's why today is 'Hobo Day' at Hypermart! In order to receive your 15% special hobo discount, simply bring a homeless person to the counter with your purchase. And remember, like every year, feminine hygiene products are not part of the 'Hobo Day' discount program. Happy shopping, and consider making a hobo part of your family today."

There were a few customers who took Jonny's announcement literally. There were a fair number of customers who complained that they couldn't find any homeless people to bring to the checkouts and other customers managed to find some. We had to implement a contingency hobo discount at 15%.

After this incident, I sat Jonny down and explained to him that he was still not being a team player. He told me that he has anger issues and I suggested that perhaps he should enter our Hypermart Behavior Modification Program. He asked for a second chance and I felt that he would get his act together at this point. I sent him home without pay.

Hardman

Hypermart ™ "Where quality is king"
677 Regent Avenue West, Winnipeg, MB R4F 6F4
Incident Report. Employee: Jonny. Status: PROBATION
March 20, 2002

Jonny has been extremely belligerent of late when asked to
clean up his cash register area. He has constructed what
can only be described as a shrine for Anthony Michael
Hall, the actor, beside his cash register. Every hour he
has been lighting a small candle and singing a strange
funeral dirge in an unrecognizable language. Not only does
this scare away customers but it is making all of his fellow employees feel quite uncomfortable. I demanded that
Jonny get rid of the shrine and cease his unusual behavior
but he claimed that he is justified in mourning "the death
of a brilliant career."

Further, Jonny stated that he has been seeking therapy
with a psychiatrist at the St. Boniface Hospital. Jonny
claimed that the doctor has assured him that he is begin-
ning to deal with his "rage issues" and that the Anthony
Michael Hall shrine is but one piece of the puzzle. We
reached a compromise by moving the shrine into the staff
room and I have requested some kind of official documenta-
tion from Jonny's psychiatrist on the matter. As he left
the office I think he called me a "fucknut."

Hardman

Hypermart ™ "Where quality is king"
677 Regent Avenue West, Winnipeg, MB R4F 6F4

Incident Report. Employee: Jonny. Status: PROBATION
November 5, 2002

Today, Jonny tackled and roughed up an elderly woman in
the front entrance of the store, beating her with her own
cane. He claims that he thought the woman was Suge Knight,
and that there was some "East Coast vs. West Coast shit
about to go down" in the store. Apparently, Jonny wasn't
wearing his contact lenses today and that was the reason
he mistook the old white woman in her seventies with a
cane for a three hundred pound black record company execu-
tive with a sawed-off shotgun. I took Jonny into my office
after Ms. Melman accepted my apologies and a $100 gift
certificate. I questioned the plausibility of his explana-
tion. No matter what I said, he kept repeating the same
phrase: "That's what THEY WANT you to think."

I told Jonny I would have to let him go. He responded by
saying "Tupac would still be alive if it wasn't for bas-
tards like you. And what of 50 cent? AND WHAT OF 50
CENT???" I told him to take the rest of the week off and
we would have a meeting with Mr. Linville to determine his
future.

Hardman

So that's that. I bled Hypermart blue and orange for over two years and yet, for whatever reason, Hardman and Linville, those two fucknut rejects from Sears, were firing my ass. Well, I wouldn't go quietly. So I stood up with my hand on my heart and I recited the words that they taught me on my very first Hypermart shift.

O Hypermart
You're in my heart
You're in my heart to stay
You welcome all
The races here
From white to black to grey
O Hypermart
You feel so good
You feel like retail love
Your prices are so very low
Thanks to the Lord above

I'M HAVING A SEIZURE, WHAT A LOVELY WAY
TO SAY I'M EPILEPTIC

I felt quite uncomfortably aroused in the soft, tacky, chocolate-brown furnishings of my girlfriend Shelby's basement. In compliance with the suburban dream, there was a fully-stocked bar in the basement and a big-screen TV. I was fifteen years old and my fifteen- year-old friends were all there. On the far end of the couch was Jeeves; his real name is Jeff, but he really liked British people. He was my closest friend. His eyes were locked on Morrissey's swaying hips. His girlfriend, Tanya, rolled her eyes in regular intervals to the music. The evil goth boy twins, Gerry and Shaun, sat symmetrically, lip-synching to "Panic" with their legs crossed, in the middle of the couch. I sprawled out on the floor and Shelby's left hand was on my crotch. *Don't come, don't come, don't come. Lanny McDonald, Ed Broadbent, Wayne Gretzky, Anne Murray, Tommy Hunter, Barbara Frum, Knowlton Nash!* Ah there, now I was less aroused — it's a good thing Canada is so very unsexy. I should remind you again that I was fifteen. I was a virgin. But I really wanted to have the sex. And I really loved this girl; Shelby was very kind and pretty; she had really cool purple hair and every Depeche Mode shirt ever made and she never seemed to mind my uncontrollable weeping. But young love was difficult for me because I was a diabetic, epileptic young man with a severe anxiety disorder. Mom and Dad were very strict as well and I think that they had implanted some sort of "neversex" chip in my brain. I had an insane amount of Non-Denominational guilt. Non-Denominational guilt is much like Catholic guilt, except you don't have to spend any "quality time" with a priest.

I had been close to making sweet love to Shelby earlier in that week but the image of my parents, speaking in tongues, praying over me to release the spirit of lust from my loins persisted. I managed to suppress my panic attack and get turned on despite this, but then another fear gripped me — the all too familiar fear of premature ejaculation. *Oh shit*, I thought. *Ummm, Al Waxman in a thong and nipple clamps, his ample chest hair glistening in the sunlight!* But I couldn't calm down. I was about to come, fully clothed, before any real heavy petting occurred. So I left Shelby's bedroom with the contrived declaration, "I'm saving myself for marriage!" and biked as far away from that potential conjugal bed as my Supercycle and feeble lungs would take me. When I began to feel dizzy and sweaty, I walked my bike toward the railway tracks, behind the ditch. I masturbated while lying on the tracks and, as I felt a train coming, I had a mild seizure, and I came. That was the day I discovered the true beauty of the epileptic orgasm. For years, I repeated this ritual over and over again — my own private version of "Towards the Last Spike." When I got home, I took a double-dose of my Tegratol, Metformin and Clonazepam. My blood sugar was a ridiculously low 3.7.

Tegratol:

Side effects I have noted: loose bowel movements, extreme fatigue and moodiness.

Metformin:

Side effects I have noted: severe nausea, general malaise, hair loss — even at my young age.

Clonazepam:

Side effects I have noted: clumsiness, laziness and slurred speech. Charming!

Anyway, I was doing all right on this night. I calmed down and Shelby's hand is no longer on my crotch. This was both a relief and a disappointment. All of us kids were watching a Cure video now, which seemed to capture our kind of adolescent angst perfectly. This was mostly due to the emotive whining of their lead singer, Robert Smith, or, as I liked to call him, "the ugliest drag queen ever." Somehow empowered by that dreadful goth droner, I decided that this was the night. I can do this. I can do Shelby, I thought. She will do me. But I had to wait for these so-called friends to leave. I was too much of a beta male to tell them to leave and I certainly couldn't drop any clever hints — that would have required a kind of social savvy beyond me. I decided on the perfect plan. I went upstairs and called my parents.

"Hello?"

"Hey Dad, umm I'm, like, over at Jeeves' place and we're having a Monopoly tournament and it's really lots of fun and Jeeves' parents said I could sleep over so ... umm, can I?"

"Son, it's Saturday night. We have church in the morning. Don't you remember? There's that special faith healer visiting from South

Bend, Indiana and he's gonna cure me of my baldness and you of your epilepsy and various other ailments."

"But Dad, I can meet you at church tomorrow morning. I really wanna …"

"Listen, you sinner, you can't sleep over! Besides, you forgot your medication at home and your mother is worried." Oh shit. My medication! "Now, I want you to get ready. I'll be there in fifteen minutes to pick you up."

CLICK.

This sucked. This really sucked. I had completely forgotten to take my medication with me. I started to feel sweaty and panicky. This really, really sucked. Jeeves lived a good fifteen minutes away by bike. Ok. I figured I could do this. I got Jeeves' keys from him and promised to leave them in his mailbox and I kissed Shelby goodbye. I got the sense from the room that everyone was mildly amused and mildly annoyed by my shame. Shelby was particularly cold. I left the house and started peddling like a bastard. I couldn't believe I forgot my meds. I couldn't believe how anxious I was right then. I started to get dizzy. The world around me was like a Wang Chung video. I was no longer on the street; I rode my bike onto a lawn, directly toward a bungalow. My brain was all strobe lights. Fuck. Jesus Christ, I was having a seizure. I tried to calm myself down in the typical manner — by singing my special seizure song to the tune of "She's Having My Baby" by Paul Anka: "I'm having a seizure! What a lovely way to say I'm epileptic!" Soon, everything was black.

I awoke in an unfamiliar kitchen and found myself surrounded by paramedics, a strange family and, of course, Mom and Dad, who stood there with their arms crossed and the most unsympathetic expressions on their faces — Mom looked like she was trying to fight off excruciating gas pain and Dad, well, Dad had a facial twitch thing going on, like he was haunted by a prison rape episode. "Well you can say goodbye to those brain cells sonny!" one of the paramedics said. And I convulsed a bit, just for effect. No sympathy. Not even from the strangers. That night, I was grounded for six months — a little bit harsh. I called Shelby's house. It must've been at least two in the morning and Jeeves answers and passes the phone to Shelby. I told her what happened. I told her how the only thing I could think of while I was going all spazzy on the ground, losing my grip on consciousness, was her, and umm, also Paul Anka. I told her how much she meant to me and how, as soon as I was no longer grounded, I would make sweet, sweet love to her. She replied by saying "I don't think it's working out, Jonny." I lost my girlfriend. I felt low. But I took a deep, wheezy breath, waited until my parents were sound asleep and headed to the train tracks. Soon, I would be sixteen — a young, diabetic, epileptic man with chronic anxiety with a driver's license and totally available. Look out ladies!

ASTHMATICA

PRO SET

Anders Anderssen

SISSY FISTS

"Behind the hill — 4 o'clock. Be there!" This was the socially accepted way to declare one's intention to fight a fellow student at Harold Hatcher Elementary School in the mid-eighties. These words were cast upon me one fateful spring day in 1985. I was in grade 2, in Ms. Bannock's Language Arts class while she was teaching us how to use the plural forms of words. This seemed to me a tedious exercise in the obvious. I had considered myself to be a fairly strong student — I was in the special spelling club, which was a kind of feeding system for the spelling bees. It was not only an honour, but a heavy responsibility. The linguistic pride of my entire class rested on a select few. And come spelling bee time, we had to step up to the plate.

I think my greatest flaw has always been my tendency toward emotional eating, but for the purposes of this story, let's just say that my greatest flaw has always been snobbery. It's not much of a stretch. Ms. Bannock noticed that that I was rolling my eyes at the seemingly futile collective Q and A session that she was conducting:

"Jimmy, what's the plural form of the word 'cow'?"

"Cows!"

"Very good Jimmy!"

I sighed. Yes, very good indeed, you mindless hick.

"Sally, what's the plural form of the word 'teacher'?"

"Ummm... Teachers?"

"Well done Sally!"

Oh way to go Sally, you singular form of hussy!

"Sven, what's the plural form of the word 'goose'?"

Oh this was a curveball! Would the new, fat Swedish kid be able to deliver? There was a long pause.

"Ummm... Geese?"

"That's right, sweetie!"

Oh Bravo, Sven, you fat, nordic god of pluralization! And "sweetie?" What the hell was that? Some God-awful pun on his ethnicity? Christ. I rolled my eyes as dramatically as I possibly could. Ms. Bannock took note of my diva behavior and directed the next question at me.

"Jonny, what's the plural form of the word 'foot'?"

"Foots!" I exclaimed instantly. I responded so quickly and thoughtlessly that I choked. Of course it was feet, what the hell was wrong with me?

As Ms. Bannock corrected me, the class erupted in laughter, slow-motion laughter. My embarrassment turned to rage as I focused on Sven Anderssen, the fat Swedish kid whose face was glowing red as he projected his grating belly laugh in my direction. Sven's yodel-like guffaws were too much to bear. I lost it.

I pointed at him and screamed "Oh yeah? Well at least I'm not a fat, dirty Swede whose father sucks at hockey."

The class grew eerily silent. Sven's father was Anders Anderssen — a recent acquisition of the Winnipeg Jets, and although he was a highly touted prospect at one point, his NHL career was a grave disappointment as he failed to adapt to the North American style of hockey. Sven's face grew redder still, and, enraged, he charged across the room and clotheslined me in the head, knocking me right off of my desk. It was quite a vicious clothesline. (If only his father could have shown that kind of determination on the ice.) Sven, Ms. Bannock and I sat in the principal's office at lunchtime. The general consensus was that I deserved an additional beating and so Mr. Rand supplemented with a light strapping. Sven got off scot-free. I knew I deserved that blow to the head. It wasn't Sven's fault that he was Swedish. No that's not it. Let me try again. It wasn't Sven's fault that he got his plural question right and I choked on mine. And it certainly wasn't his fault that his father was a sub-par leftwinger. I was ready to bury the hatchet and move on when Sven approached me during the afternoon recess and made the announcement.

"Behind the hill — 4 o'clock. Be there!"

The hill behind our school was not so much a hill as it was a grass-covered speedbump. Its elevation was due entirely to the fact that it used to be a landfill. The city planners just tossed some sod over the garbage like a throw rug and our hill was born.

A huge group of kids convened behind the hill, pumping their fists and chanting "Sven! Sven! Sven!" He had a posse of older tough kids who were giving him some last-minute pointers. I shuffled down the hill by myself. I know I couldn't escape this. The sheer spectacle of it all was intimidation enough, not to mention the clearly pro-Sven crowd. And then there was Sven, rosy cheeked and pumped up, like a chubby miniature version of Dolph Lundgren. I was so screwed.

We circled each other, with Sven occasionally kicking at the air between us, and me waving my dukes around like a fop attempting to adhere to Marquis of Queensbury rules. The comedic value of our prancing was short-lived and the crowd was getting restless. The chants of Sven's name began to peter out and people began to disperse as we continued to circle each other like mentally challenged square dancers. Eventually, there was a smaller, less partisan crowd, and they had grown impatient with Sven's lack of killer instinct. I was able to implement my only strategy to get out of this. As much as snobbery was my fault, oratory was my gift. I raised my hand and addressed the crowd.

"My dear and worthy opponent, fellow classmates, I propose that violence is not the solution to our problem. Let us instead drink the sweet nectar of forgiveness. For, is not the sweetest drink, the drink shared with friends? Sven, I apologize for my behavior earlier today. It was wrong to transfer my shame into verbal aggression towards you. We can all learn from my mistake. Your father is a highly-skilled hockey player. Please send him my regards. And please, do accept my apology, my fair-haired, portly, fiord-navigating, Nordic compadre."

I reached out my hand. After a pause, he took it. There we stood, in the middle of the field behind that famed hill of violence, shaking hands. It was a cinematic moment to say the least. Those left of the bloodthirsty crowd were not particularly pleased. They called us "sissies." I tightened my grip on Sven's hand and kneed him in the groin; as he was doubled over I began to pound on him mercilessly. The crowd was now clearly on my side. "Jonny! Jonny! Jonny!" It may have been a dirty way to win a fight but it does speak to the power of a persuasive speech. Besides, his father had played 57 games with the Jets that year and scored 5 goals, with 13 assists, for a total of 18 points with 20 penalty minutes. I felt I was pounding on him on behalf of many disenfranchised Jets fans. I spent the next few minutes kicking Sven in the stomach, working him over with both of my foots.

Anders Anderssen — Career Statistics
Height: 5'10, Weight: 175, Shoots: Left.

Hartford Whalers (NHL)

	GP	G	A	PTS	PIM
1986	66	14	20	34	14

Winnipeg Jets (NHL)

	GP	G	A	PTS	PIM
1987	58	9	25	34	10
1988	57	5	13	18	20

In the off-season, Anders is an avid dog-racing enthusiast.

PREVIOUSLY ENJOYED CROSSWORDS

Dear Reader,

You're probably bored by now. God knows I am. So, for the next few pages, why don't you relax, take off your clothes and take a gander at these previously enjoyed, freestyle, fake crosswords. They're wicked awesome!

Love,
JPF

"Jon Paul Fiorentino Fever"

Across 1. Sequel to *Asthmatica*. 9. "_____ to your asthma." 10. JPF's literary designation. 11. JPF derives his sexual power from this shellfish. 12. Idiotic Italian soccer star. 13. Preferred drug at raves. 14. JPF's mentor. 15. Phoneme cousin. 19. JPF enjoys breathing this. 24. JPF's most notable characteristic (American spelling). 27. JPF's second most notable characteristic. 28. JPF has three of these.

Down: 1. JPF's first love? 2. Hemorrhoid soother. 3. JPF's nickname in high school. 4. Funky_____. 5. JPF is always this way with his fans (all three of them). 6. Often declared by women in JPF's company. 7. JPF unsuccessfully tried out for this *Facts of Life* role. 8. JPF asked Santa for this implant. 14. JPF's arch nemesis, Jewel, at times. 16. JPF prefers to use this term when referring to syphilis. 17. JPF suffered this injury while writing *Resume Drowning*. 18. Synonym for one down. 20. JPF's favourite direction. 21. Graham wafer treat that JPF will never enjoy because of his crippling diabetes. 25. JPF's real father.

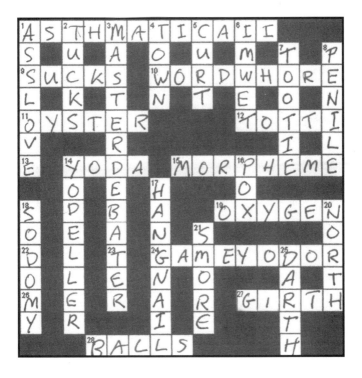

"Can Lit Fever"

Across

1. Name of Margaret Laurence fanzine. 3. Rite of Passage in Toronto literary scene. 9. W.P. Kinsella needs ten a day. 10. City outside of Brampton. 18. Robbie Burns classic. 21. Douglas Coupland's passion. 23. Lorna Crozier organization. 24. Coach House artifact. 25. Trope appearing in every Canadian text. 26. Humourist pleasure prolonger. 27. Alice Munro's charge.

Down

1. Birthplace of poet Burton Cummings. 2. Birthplace of poet Avril Lavigne. 4. Harmful to albinos. 5. bill bissett guarantee. 6. Kingston literary group. 7. Author of Auld Lang Syne. 8. Seven down's problem. 11. Seven down's blood type. 15. Tom Jones' Can Lit classic. 16. Timothy Findley's friend, perhaps? 17. Type of lab in Rob Mclennan's basement. 19. Advisor to Leonard Cohen. 20. Component of psyche that is in complete control of Michael Winter. 23. Response to "Are you familiar with the works of Gabrielle Roy?"

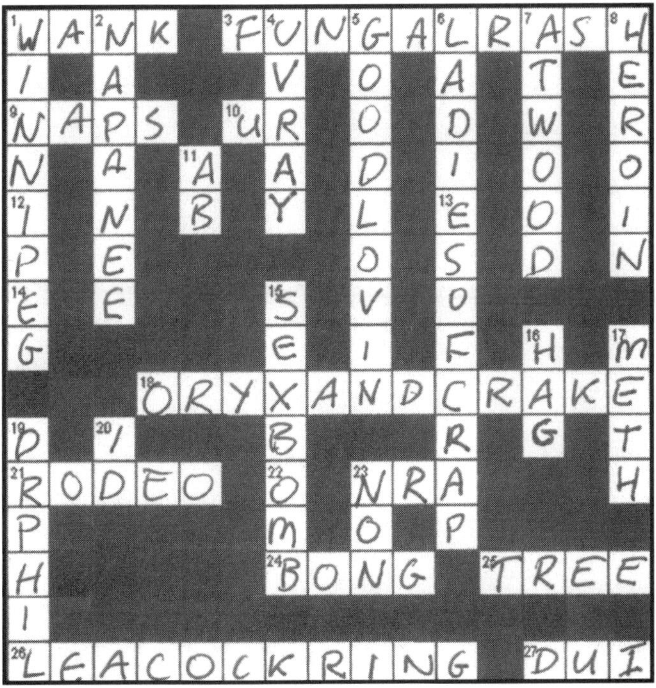
WANK FUNGALRASH
I A V O A T E
NAPS UR O D W R
N A A A D I O O
I N B Y L E O I
P E O S D N
E E S V O
G E I F H M
ORYXANDCRAKE
D I B R G T
RODEO O NRA H
P M O P
H BONG TREE
I
LEACOCKRING DUI

ASTHMATICA PRO SET

Mom

MILKMAN

It was the Milkman's first shift. The whistled tune of "Close to You" by The Carpenters dispersed from between his lips and into the cool, still suburban air. His sparkling white shirt and slacks and matching sparkling white cap fit perfectly into the Redonda Street scene. The sun greeted him. The smell of recently cut grass filled his nostrils and the pastel pink and baby blue bungalows welcomed him with their front entrance lights. In the distance, two boys frolicked at the bottom of the hill behind the elementary school.

*

I would meet Lee at the foot of the hill in the early morning before Harold Hatcher Elementary School would open its doors and allow the children of Transcona to breathe in its asbestos. We would meet while the streetlights were slowly nodding off and the sky blossomed into yellow and violet. We would wrestle and bound up the hill and tumble down and challenge each other's egos. One time, Lee rammed my head into the left field foul pole of the baseball diamond that stretched from the bottom of the hill to Redonda Street where the school rested. The next day, I took a handful of sand from the very same baseball diamond and crammed it down the front of Lee's pants. Lee was eleven and I was ten. We were best friends.

"Your Mother is a dirty hooker!" Lee said, his voice crackling.

"Guidance counsellor!" I responded.

"Whatever!" Lee grabbed my left nipple, twisted it and we frolicked for a while before Lee broke out the Lysol. Huffing was an integral part of our friendship. I didn't partake in the solvent abuse, I was too scared. I did enable Lee though — I would hold his long, flowing, blond hair as he huffed. Early on, Lee had discovered the economical joy of recreational solvent use and, for him, it always helped to pass a long and tedious school day.

*

Once, Lee had me over for milk and cookies. We sat at the kitchen table as if we were posing for Norman Rockwell. Lee's mother waddled toward us and placed two glasses of milk on the table. "Nice, cold, refreshing milk," she proclaimed as she patted our heads simultaneously. Lee gulped the milk down swiftly and smirked at me as I fidgeted in my seat.

"Hey, ass? Why don't you drink your milk?" he asked.

"I'm not an ass. I don't think I'm allowed to drink milk, Lee."

"What are you talking about stupid? My mom says all growing boys need milk! And why did you agree to come over for milk and cookies if you're not allowed to drink milk?"

"I thought 'milk and cookies' was a figure of speech. And I'm not supposed to drink milk cause my mom says I'm allergic and stuff."

"Allergic? Jesus, Jonny! You can't be allergic! Nobody is allergic to sweet, tasty, wholesome milk! Listen, your mom is a stupid, useless, dirty so-called 'guidance counsellor' and you don't even really know who your dad is. I think I know what I'm talking about here."

Lee's mother rushed through the kitchen on her way to do some ironing. "Don't listen to him, Jonny dear. Your mom may be a skank, but she is very hygienic."

For some reason, Lee had always been convinced that my mother was a "lady of the night." Even though Mom held a very respectable position of guidance counsellor at Murdoch MacKay Collegiate Institute, he was certain that I was the product of an extra-marital trick-turning episode.

I felt the weight of the world on my shoulders. Lee wouldn't stop staring at me with a scornful look. My lips inched toward the glass. I took a sip of trepidation and looked up at Lee earnestly. Lee smirked, "See Jonny? You are an ass." I began to gulp it down. "You know, Jonny my man? You should really listen to me more often. Allergic to milk! That's just plain ridiculous." After a good five minutes of post-gloating silence, Lee watched as I clenched the back of my pants and writhed around the floor, purple-faced and panic-stricken. The AM radio crackled in the background with the melodious strains of The Carpenters.

*

I was convinced that Lee was cruel to me because his dad was cruel to him. Mom told me it was indicative of a cycle of verbal abuse: "Lee and his father are participating in a spiral of hurt. It affects the wellness of everyone involved. I pray for their spiritual health every night," she would say. Lee's dad was a boorish man. He worked as a financial advisor in one of those big buildings downtown. I witnessed Lee's dad's cruelty once when I was a dinner guest. We had TV dinners and were gathered around the television, watching *ALF*. Lee and I were really into the show and Lee's mom was really into her dinnertime Colt 45, but Lee's dad was trying to impart some wisdom to his son.

"You see Lee, my boy, the key to the market is to buy low and sell high. But you have to stay away from these new fad stocks like IBM," Mr Johnson began.

Lee was completely fixated on that furry, wisecracking alien and did not pay attention to his dad at all. Mr. Johnson grew annoyed.

"Hey! Pay attention you little shit!"

"Sorry Dad. I was just watching ..."

In the episode, ALF was wrongfully accused of eating the Tanner family cat, Lucky. It was highly entertaining, and Lee could not be faulted for being seduced by the comedic genius of that furry alien. I, too, was mesmerized.

"What the hell is with you and your little bastard friend? Is he your boyfriend or something? I mean, Goddamn it boy! Why do you hang around with 'delicate' kids like that?"

Mrs. Johnson chirped in to correct Mr. Johnson, "Now, now dear, Jonny may be a disgusting little sissy, but he does mean well."

"Thanks, Mrs. J," I said.

"Would you two do me a favour and shut your word holes?" Mr. Johnson bellowed. Then he addressed Lee, "Now, young man, you listen to me. You're never going to get ahead in this world by fraternizing with the 'homeowners' of the world. They don't deserve respect. Your little pal Jonny is gonna end up carousing with Elton John and Rip Taylor. You need to spend your time with kids who have less sinful vices, like ... erm ... tax evasion. You have to make connections Lee. It's the only way to succeed in life."

"Yes Dad."

"Now there's a good boy. Now pass the milk."

Lee took a swig and passed it on.

*

Lee would come round my house to fetch me quite often. This particular morning, he stood under my open bedroom window chanting "Milkman! Milkman!" I was busy combing my My Little Pony doll, and singing the My Little Pony jingle: "My Little Pony, pretty pony, I love to brush your hair."

Lee hucked a rock through the open window and pegged me on the head. I was enraged. I threw my My Little Pony against the wall. "Why didn't you protect me, Ambrosia? God, you are such a prick."

"Let me in!" Lee bellowed from the street below.

"Coming," I sighed.

My home decor was made up of wall-to-wall orange shag carpet, velvet paintings of Jesus and various out-of-season nativity scenes. Lee followed me into my room. I remained silent. I flung myself onto my bed and cuddled up to my Cheer Bear.

"It's not my fault that you're lactating!" Lee chirped.

"I'm lactose intolerant. It means I'm allergic to milk — just like my mom said, just like I told you!"

"Ok. Fine. But you can't blame me. You're the sick freak with the weird illness. Who ever heard of being allergic to milk?"

"I guess it's a little weird."

"You're damn right it's weird!" Lee gently punched me in the shoulder.

I giggled. "Stop it, you ass!"

We rolled around for a while on the bed, pinching and biting each other affectionately and then Lee began to wax philosophical: "You know the only one we can truly blame for this unfortunate mishap?

"Who?"

A perverse smile crept onto Lee's face. He leapt to his feet and began to pace with his arms folded behind his back.

"Well, we know for a fact that your mother is not a lactating immigrant."

"Lactose intolerant!"

"Whatever. She's not allergic to milk right?

"Right. She drinks milk all the time. She loves its creamy goodness."

"Now, it is a fact that you have no idea who your father is right?"

I sighed. "Lee, my dad is downstairs right now, playing Bible Trivia with my mom."

"Come now, my dear boy. Logically, we can assume that your so-called 'father' has never made love to a woman. And even if he managed to somehow sire you, that would mean he would have to be allergic to milk. Is he?"

I raised an eyebrow. "No."

"Now, obviously, being allergic to milk is quite rare. No offense, Jonny but you are a genetic freak."

"I guess so."

"Tell me something Jonny, my man, If you were hiring a milkman, you wouldn't want him to steal any milk right?"

"Yeah. I suppose, but I don't ..."

"Woah. Slow down cowboy! Just stay with me here!"

"Ok."

"Ok ... If I were the milkman, Christ knows that I would drink a great deal of milk because milk is so goddamned tasty. And I would probably drink the milk company right out of business."

"Yeah. You really like milk."

"So tell me this then, my dear Jonny, wouldn't the best possible milkman be a guy who, for some ghastly reason, couldn't enjoy the frothy, wholesome goodness of milk. Perhaps someone who was ALLERGIC TO MILK?"

"Do you think I should be a milkman?"

"No, you idiot. Jonny, the milkman is your father! Your FATHER! He's the reason you're such a sad, lactating mutant! And he doesn't even have the guts to take responsibility for his poor, poor, stupid son. I'm telling you that milkman son of a bitch is to blame for all of this. He's to blame for your very existence!"

"Oh my God! That bastard!"

"Actually, technically you're the bastard, Jonny. But still we can't let this evil milkman get away with this!" Lee took a deep breath of satisfaction. He paused for a moment and looked deep into my eyes. "Milkman!" he said.

"Milkman!" I repeated.

Lee left my room and I sat on the corner of my bed, contemplating the gravity of the situation. After I picked up Ambrosia and placed her back on the headboard, I started down the hallway. As I turned the corner, I glimpsed Lee and my mom hugging. Lee was sobbing: "I'm a good boy right?"

"Of course you are, sweetie. Of course you are."

I quietly retreated to my room. Poor Lee. All he needed was some sweet mom love.

*

Early morning. We stealthily crept into the back of the milk truck. Lee opened up two cartons of milk and took mighty swigs from each of them. Then we inserted our penises into our respective cartons and topped them up. As the Milkman continued his route, so did we continue our subtle pursuit. As the noble milk servant of the people strode up and down the sidewalks of Transcona, blissfully humming a popular tune, a faint, haunting whisper began to emanate from the shrubs and the backyards of homes. "Milkman! Milkman!" Our voices resonated, as if possessed by some unholy spirit. Our whispered chant grew louder as the milkman's shift lingered on. "Milkman! Milkman!" The town seemed to grow static before the diligent worker's eyes. The sun refused to rise. He peered into the bushes in front of 189 Allenby Crescent where he perceived the incantation to be coming from. As he approached the bushes, sinister, guttural and disembodied voices croaked in unison "MILKMAN!" The shrubs seemed to lurch forward and the milkman yelped and retreated to the milk truck with inhuman speed. As he turned around, now safely behind the wheel of his truck, he saw two shadows dart across the crescent under faint streetlight. The early morning was filled with the chilling laughter of two very stupid boys.

SPECIAL FEATURE: *MILKMAN* (DELETED SCENE)

Jonny

Lee
(Angrily)

Jonny
(Confused)

Lee
(Convincingly)

Jonny
(Astonished)

END SCENE

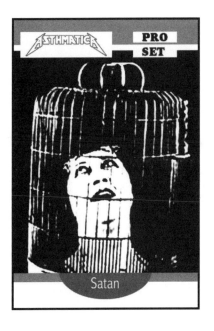

HAIL, SATAN

I remember the taxi very well. It was the first time a taxi had ever pulled up to our house. In fact, it was very odd to see a taxi in Transcona at all — the people who lived in Transcona couldn't afford taxis (my family was one of the few exceptions) nor were the taxi drivers clamouring to get that all important white trash fare. The taxi was for my older brother, Jamie. He had called my parents on their bluff and now he was leaving. I was so impressed. He was leaving home before getting kicked out of the house. I really wanted his room, but more importantly, I wanted to move up in the family from tertiary male to secondary male. I was fourteen and I was filling out quite nicely. I figured that within two years, I would be able to fight Dad and win. And then I could take Mom far away, to Saskatchewan to deprogram her. I had already beaten Dad at chess once, although I think he may have let me win. The dispute was really between Dad and my brother and no one else. Jamie was to dispose of the Ozzy Osbourne and Black Sabbath cassette tapes or face the consequences of being a sixteen-year-old hobo.

Mom and I took our respective sympathetic positions. She would say things to Jamie like "Your father is just concerned for your spiritual health. He wants you to serve the Lord, not swerve from the Lord."

And I would say things to Jamie like "Dude, you are so in the right. I think you should blast that Sabbath even louder just to spite him. Besides, Ozzy's just using devil worship as a metaphor — he's really singing about corporate greed ... man."

To each of us, my brother would respond with a crackling voice: "Screw you, Mom," or "screw you, Jon."

I really did admire my brother. It was mostly his attitude that I held in high regard. That whole *I'm not gonna listen to your fascist rules, man* thing was very effective and dramatic. His fashion sense, however, was a different story. He wore this acid-wash jean jacket with an Iron Maiden patch on the back, black or blue jeans with a tight roll at the bottom; or sometimes he would tuck his jeans into his hi-top running shoes. He had full braces with these bright blue elastic bands hooked from the top teeth to the bottom. I fully understood that the braces were necessary, but really. His mullet would be worshipped in certain hyper-ironic fashion oeuvres of today; but, to me, it was ghastly. (To this day, I carry around a wallet-size school photo of Jamie circa grade 10. Just looking at that metal-mouthed picture of teenage awkwardness is enough to cure the most abject case of the blues.)

The metallic navy blue taxi with automatic transmission and power steering idled in our driveway as my brother whipped the Tipper Gore book, *Raising PG Kids in an X-Rated Society*, at Dad, who was, at this point, quite flustered. He was losing this showdown. It seemed that with every passing day, Dad was losing more and more. This was both sad and exciting. I pictured myself when I was sixteen pulling off a more subtle and fashionable version of this drama:

Dad, if you can't live with the fact that your son is taken by the theories of Michel Foucault and the music of Air Supply, then you are just going to have to let me spread my wings and fly! For now, the adolescent angst stage was all Jamie's and he played his part like a wily veteran.

"How are you supposed to make a living looking like that?" Dad asked.

"I'm gonna rock, old man. Rock is the only thing worth living for!" he responded. This was amazing! Go Jamie! "You'll never know what it means to rock. R-O-C-K! You gots to give it your all. It's either balls out or tits up ... dude!"

"Don't use that language under my roof," Dad said.

Mom was crying and praying aloud quite obnoxiously from the master bedroom: "Please Jesus! Pleeeeeaaaassse!"

The truth was, Jamie was already very close to making a living. He had been playing the piano at the Royal Fork Buffet for tips. As the locals stuffed their faces with second and third helpings of roasted "chicken" and synthetic ice cream, he would play up-tempo versions of "Ballerina Girl" in order to pick up the pace of their gorging. He helped move the crowd quickly. He was well loved at the Royal Fork. He wore the long part of his "shortlong" in a ponytail. This was a concession he would never make at home. I had stumbled upon my brother's newly found vocation accidentally when my grade 8 chess club had its annual banquet at the Royal Fork. There he was, wearing a shiny, grey, speckled suit with a black and white piano key patterned tie, tickling the ivories like a sedated bastard.

The reigning chess champion, let's call him Lou Gossett Jr. just for fun, snorted and yelped "Hey Jonny, isn't that your brother up there? What a loser!"

"Shut up, Lou Gossett Jr."

He continued to taunt me and I tried to ignore him and remained hunched over my potato salad. What a dreadful situation — to be mocked by the grand master of Arthur Day Junior High chess. I was never really into the chess; I just needed friends and I felt like I could instill some fashion sense within these horrid, oily-faced kids. I failed in both of my endeavors. My brother never noticed me and as we left the restaurant, I heard an almost unrecognizable muzak version of "Crazy Train." He was being subversive — he just couldn't stop the rock.

The cab began to pull away from my house without my brother in it. He was trying to get down the stairs but Dad was blocking his way, reading aloud from the Bob Larson book, *Satanism: The Seduction of America's Youth*. "Christians awake! ..." My brother juked left and went right, getting past Dad, bursting toward the front door. The taxi was halfway down the street and my brother clutched his duffel bag and sprinted after the car in vain. My parents and I stood on the front porch watching him as he gradually slowed down and sucked on his ventolin. He didn't look back; he just continued on toward the bus stop. We don't have much in common, but I do love my big brother. Despite this concession, I don't think I could ever love him as much as I did the day he chased that propane-fuelled Olds Cutlass Supreme #145 taxi down our dusty little Transcona street. That was the day he didn't look back; that was the day I scored my dream bedroom. Thanks, Satan!

STRAPPING YOUNG LADS

In every childhood, there is a box. The box of which I speak is usually found in the parents' closet or the basement or the attic; it either contains something you were hoping to never see in your parents' possession (like pot, GHB, or pornography) or it contains something you were desperately looking for (like pot, GHB, or pornography). My parents, being so chummy with Jesus and all, were pretty clean living. Despite this, I was always on the prowl for something cheeky. The closest I ever came to finding pornography in the house, was a book in Dad's night table drawer entitled *A Christian's Guide to Coupling*. This book had chapter titles such as "Why Sodom Burned," "Foreplay is for Sinners" and "Finding 'the Jesus Spot.'" Needless to say, it wasn't particularly arousing (but I learned to make due). In my seemingly endless quest for sexually explicit material, I stumbled on a few curiosities — homemade wine and beer kits, Amway catalogues, costume jewellery. But I had never encountered anything particularly explicit until I found the box.

My box was different than yours. Not better, just different and quite possibly worse. I found the box after school one afternoon in the basement. The box was of the generic cardboard variety and it lay underneath a bunch of other similar boxes, behind the water heater. I had done my rounds in this part of the basement before but I hadn't noticed this particular box. It looked as if it had been recently placed at the bottom of the stack, on purpose. I cleared away the other boxes, swiftly, yet carefully so as to not alert my folks upstairs of my detective work. The box was filled with worn-out leather straps — at least twenty of them. Half of them were cracked down the middle; some had lost their colour; others were considerably thinner on one end.

Dad was the principal of the toughest high school in Transcona and it was no secret to me that he was a stern man, but for some reason, my discovery threw me for a loop. Eventually it made sense. I could just see him late at night, sneaking downstairs, and breaking open the box to reminisce, stroking each strap — "Ah, Good Ol' Strappy. I remember breaking you on little Richie Anderson. That was some swollen behind, eh Strappy? Oh, Strappy, you were such a good, sturdy strap."

I began to visit the box of straps on a regular basis, after school. Holding the dulled leather in my hand, I would let my imagination run wild. I imagined myself as the delinquent student, stealing a bike, smoking dope behind the school, putting a cherry bomb in the toilet. I occasionally lightly strapped my own hands, arms and ass. Looking back at my quality time with the box, I realize that each strap symbolized the auspicious work of many students.

In my eleventh year, I became a problem child. I began sneaking out of the house after my curfew of 7pm to play street hockey with friends. The most shocking part about this development was that I had friends. I would stash my stick at Robbie's house and when the snowball hit my window, that was my signal to squeeze my portly frame out of my second-storey window and navigate the icy shingles of the garage roof and land safely on the snowbank in my front yard. I knew that my parents would eventually catch me. But, for the moment, I took comfort in the fact that they held Bible studies almost every weeknight and were more than likely too busy speaking in tongues to notice my absence.

One December night, after a rowdy game of street hockey, I was about to hoist myself up onto the roof from the snowbank, carefully gripping the eavestroughs between the dancing blue and white Christmas lights when the front door opened and Dad, who was in the midst of bidding adieu to one of his fellow parishioners, locked eyes with me. Fear shot through me — I slipped, fell on the snowbank and looked up at him. His bottom lip was quivering and I had a feeling he wasn't being overcome with the Holy Spirit.

"What the hell are you doing?" he said. His fellow Bible studier appeared shocked at his choice of phrase. Dad quickly let his Christian brother go. "Pardon my language, Bill. I'll see you tomorrow night. Right now, I have to administer some Old Testament love to my disobedient son here. You know: spare the rod, spoil the child."

"Righto, chief. I hear that. If there's one thing I know, it's that God compels us to beat the crap out of our children — that's for sure," Bill said, and scurried off to his beige Plymouth K-Car.

I thought Mom and Dad might be happy that I managed to find a social life despite all of the restrictions and odds against me. But Mom was relatively silent, save for a few "shame on yous" and Dad was relentless. I was spanked into another dimension. And as he spanked my bare ass raw, I cranked my neck back to catch a glimpse of his beet-red face. Sweat was pouring off the top of his rapidly-balding head. I couldn't stop thinking about some disturbing things: first, will I suffer the same fate as Dad? In the future, might there be some wonderful, magical tonic to combat male pattern baldness? And, also, why wasn't he using a strap? This was the first time since my discovery that I had been on the receiving end of corporal punishment. And it occurred to me now that he had never bothered to use one of his precious straps on me. Sure I was wooden spoon, belt and fist worthy. But what about the provincially approved educational strap? Was I not strap worthy?

I took my punishment and subsequent grounding with great bitterness although I did not say a word. Instead, I devised a response that would be much more powerful than words.

Three days before Christmas, my parents went out for the afternoon to a spiritual recovery seminar, my brother was supposed to look after me but, the moment my parents left, he was out the door to hang out with his headbanger friends and worship Satan. I got to work immediately. I hauled the box of straps up from the basement and covered it with as much wrapping paper as I could find. I put a large red bow on it and a gift tag: "To: Dad, From: Santa."

Dad was very excited by the mystery present under the tree. Mom was completely amazed. "What wonderful boys you have! Isn't that right dear?" she squealed.

"They're a blessing, honey. An absolute blessing!"

I responded with a coquettish smile, and my brother simply remained indifferent, which served my purposes perfectly.

Christmas morning came and the presents were exchanged. I got the complete New Testament action figure set and a couple of Christian *Archie* comics. The Christian *Archie* comics were very much like the regular *Archie* comics, except the Riverdale gang spent less time dating and hanging out at the Malt Shoppe, and more time judging heathens. We decided as a family to save Dad's mystery present for last. He tugged and clawed at the wrapping paper, layer after layer. As he peeled away the final layer, the expression on his face shifted from anticipation to abjection to anger. He gripped Good Ol' Strappy and held her high over his head. I smiled. Now I was gonna get it. Finally. But what was this? Dad was staring Jamie down!

"What kind of sick joke is this, you Devil-worshipping bastard! You are not my son!"

"Hey, don't pin this on me, man," Jamie said.

"Yeah," I added, "It was my ..."

"Don't protect your brother!" Dad bellowed, as he lunged forward and chased Jamie thoughout the house, eventually cornering him and giving Good Ol' Strappy one last swat at glory.

As I watched Jamie get the leather laid to him, and I witnessed the sheer intensity of the beating, I realized that maybe it wasn't all that important to be deemed strap worthy. I decided not to protest or take responsibility for the gift. After all, I knew that whatever Jamie was receiving from Dad, I would receive from Jamie shortly after. It was the best Christmas ever!

Eventually, the box made its way back down to the basement, this time further concealed by stacks of hymnals and inspirational novels. And as I awkwardly trudged toward teenagehood, I made it a habit to revisit the box every time I transgressed (you know typical preteen hijinks: taking the Lord's name in vain, thinking impure thoughts, saying grace improperly, stuff like that). My visits were my way of saying "me too" to both the legends of delinquency and to those who administered their sentences.

ASTHMATICA PRO SET

Great Aunt Becky

SICKER QUICKER

"Keep your eyes on the road, you stupid fuck," my Great Aunt Becky said.

But my eyes were on the road — just not the road directly in front of me. The wheels were whipping gravel up in my face. My head was completely out of the window and I left a spectacular trail of vomit in my wake. I kept one hand on the steering wheel and slid my head back into my awesome light blue 1981 Chevrolet Chevette carefully so as to not ruin the lush, burgundy, vinyl upholstery. "Calm down, honey," I responded, quickly realizing that I should probably not refer to my Great Aunt Becky as "honey." I let it go. We were both so very drunk and stoned. I looked at the speedometre — only five kilometres over the speed limit. Sweet.

"You drive like your sissy father, you silly bitch!"

"Jesus, Great Aunt Becky. Why don't you take the wheel then?"

"No way. I'm too fucked up."

The message of the night seemed very clear: don't go cruising with your Great Aunt Becky after drinking a two-four of Labatt

Maximum Ice and dropping acid with her. Especially not on a school night.

We decided to drive around after a night of bingo at the Transcona Legion. We drove through the back roads of St. Vital, trying to avoid the cops, talking smack to each other and eventually puking.

For a long time, Great Aunt Becky was my entire teenage life. She was a shrewd woman — a true sociopath who by day was a devout Christian, and by night, an insatiable substance abuser who showed me the psychotropic ropes and taught me how to drive drunk. One minute she would be in the living room, engaged in bible study, faking the ability to speak in tongues: "Abbballahmallah Himininin Allabi!" and the next, smoking weed with me behind the garage: "Remember Jonny, always save your roaches. You never know when you'll need an emergency 'wake and bake.'"

Now, as we rounded a sharp corner, it was Great Aunt Becky's turn to puke as she disgracefully poked her head out of the window and began to hurl. Why was it that I could never outlast Great Aunt Becky? I always puked first. I guess she was the old pro. She quickly recovered, rolled up her window, tilted her head toward me and smiled. Good old Great Aunt Becky. Then a second wave of vomit came and her instincts took over: she bashed her head on the closed window and then let it fly all over the rough draft of my Walt Whitman essay which she had been proofreading.

"Goddamn it, Great Aunt Becky, you bastard! My essay! My upholstery! My fucking brilliant Walt Whitman essay! That was my only copy!"

"It's still readable."

I pulled over and snatched it out of her hands. "No it's not!"

"Well, maybe it's for the best, dear. It was a pretty shitty essay."

"What? I argue that the Whitmanian poetic oeuvre is plagued with the anxiety of a latent heterosexuality! It's a very original thesis."

"It's horseshit, kid."

"Asshole."

I peered through the bug-splattered windshield and saw the empty street that provided us with our obscure way home. I began to long for home. I began to feel more and more sober. Stupid Great Aunt Becky.

"Hey! Your face looks like a cantaloupe. It's cantaloupe-esque! It's cantaloupian!" Great Aunt Becky said, sounding all of a sudden, like Barbara Walters.

"Barbara, you are tripping hard," I said, doing my best Hugh Downs.

"Maybe so, cantaloupe boy, but if I have to, I WILL cut you," Great Aunt Becky said, brandishing her Swiss Army knife.

"Dude, Great Aunt Becky! That's so not cool."

"Whatever."

The car grew silent. I took an inventory of the evening. Great Aunt Becky and I snuck in a few Maximum Ice into the Legion because they only serve Labatt Lite during bingo and you might as well drink rainwater if you're gonna drink that. So, we met up with Grandma and we all got pretty loaded as we sat there and lost game after game. Bingo performance anxiety eventually set in and Great Aunt Becky and I ditched Grandma and hooked up with Uncle Floyd in the parking lot of the Transcona Non-Denominational Church. Uncle Floyd was nobody's uncle as far as we knew but he did grope you like an uncle if you got too close. His face was always shiny from a constant layer of sweat. He smelled like a mixture of an abandoned gym locker and a janitor's mop bucket. Everyone knew that Uncle Floyd was the town pervert, an equal opportunity fondler; but there was something very endearing about Uncle Floyd — his drug supply. Uncle Floyd prided himself on the quality and quantity of his drugs (as well as his mint condition *Bop* and *Tiger Beat* magazines). We scored two licks of acid each from Uncle Floyd and escaped relatively unfondled to the Chevette.

Now, as I drove past the trailer park, I wondered why it was that I always got sicker quicker than Great Aunt Becky. It was clear from her refusal to drive, her inability to understand who knocks up whom, her vomit all over my brilliant Walt Whitman essay, that I was the rational one, the one in control. But Great Aunt Becky always managed to outlast me in the vomit category. As I continued to muse on this injustice, Great Aunt Becky began to espouse her wisdom on the art of drunk driving: "You see, my dear foppish nephew, the key to an artful and successful drunk driving experience is to feel the burn, to keep your eyes on the prize if you will. For, we all know that one has to be in it to win it..." All of a sudden, blue and red lights flashed across my windshield. Cops!

"Fucking piggy cops!" Great Aunt Becky said with glee. This is where Great Aunt Becky really shone. I put on my special driving goggles and toyed with the cops for a few blocks. You can only push a 1981 Chevrolet Chevette so far, so I eventually pulled over and let Great Aunt Becky do her thing. Within minutes, she was leg wrestling the policeman on the hood of the squad car and the burly officer was effectively pinned and out fifty bucks just like that.

We reached my street at four that morning, after doing some night-cap Jager shots with the emasculated officer. I crept into the drive-way, with the car lights turned off. I asked Great Aunt Becky if she could help me rewrite my Walt Whitman essay. But her seat was fully reclined and she was fast asleep on my essay. I tried to yank the essay free but she kept biting my hand. I left her to sleep it off. Stupid Great Aunt Becky.

REJECTED ESSAY TITLES

My Bum is On Your Lips: Marshall Mathers and the Illocutionary Speech Act

The Ap(parent) Trap of the Sentence: The Olsen Twins, Charles Olson and the Trappings of Syntax

Wesley and Bosie — Two Angry Jung Men: A Psychosexual Approach to Mr. Wilde and Mr. Belvedere

Hey! You! Get Into My Car!: The Hegemonic Naming Act of Billy Ocean

Whatcha Talkin' bout Hillis?: Gary Coleman and the American Post-Structural

Too Many Colons: The Colonized Text and a Postcolonial Approach to Colonoscopy

Luck Be a Post-Structuralist Feminist Tonight: Cixous as the Chairman of the Broad

Please Sir, May I Have Some Mouré?: The Language Poetry of Charles Dickens

You Know What Really Gets My Goat?: Overused Idioms in English

Penetrating the Alligator Pie: R. Kelly Reads Dennis Lee

I See London, I See France, I Hate my Life: The Curse of Jon Paul Fiorentino

LOOKAGE

The Winnipeg Arena did not have individual urinals. It had pissing troughs. You had to piss against a wall of flowing water that carried your urine into the collective piss ether. The Winnipeg Arena, former home of the Winnipeg Jets, is where I, at the age of ten, first encountered the horror of lookage. The Jets were trailing the Hartford Whalers 3-2 early in the second period. I went to the pissing trough, where a tubby, bearded hockey dad straddled up and pissed right beside me despite the ample room on either side of us. Around halfway through my stream, I heard the roar of the crowd. We had tied it up and I missed the goal. I frowned and re-focused on the task at/in hand when I noticed that the hockey dad was staring directly at my pre-pubescent package. He spoke softly and hauntingly. "Sounds like we scored, eh squirt? Can I buy you a beer? I wouldn't mind scoring myself." I panicked and bolted, spraying urine on the floor and my pants.

Once, when I was around twelve, I was guilty of lookage. My father took me to a Jets game a mere two days after having a vasectomy. I wasn't quite sure what a vasectomy was but my brother, Jamie, had me convinced that my father had had his manhood surgically removed. I did not know exactly what was lost, but I did assume the worst. It was an afternoon game and our Jets were playing the

Quebec Nordiques. As he gimped his way to his seat, I remember thinking how ridiculous he looked, and then later, how brave it was of him to take me to that game despite his recent loss of "man power." Inevitably, he had to take a leak — the Labatt Blue will have that effect — so I helped him down the stairs and we made our way to the washroom and the trough. As we simultaneously let the whiz fly, I heard a high-pitched yelp of pain come from my father. I glanced over at his face and I saw a grimace that I will never forget. His eyes were shut tightly, and his bottom teeth were digging into his upper lip. He was in the midst of a titanic struggle. With every last drip and shake, the after-effect of the vasectomy was pelting him with sharp pangs. He should have been in bed, heavily medicated. I just had to glance and see that it was still there, and if not, where was he pissing from? To my surprise, he was still a man, still intact. The only evidence of my father's lost manhood was auditory — the girlish shrieking that continued to echo throughout the men's washroom. All of a sudden, my psychological struggle with the pissing trough seemed simply ridiculous. I had finished but I couldn't take my eyes off of my poor father, as he slowly zipped up and turned to me to say "Don't run off on me Jonny, help Daddy back to his seat." I would not have been surprised to instead hear him say "Help Daddy back to the car." But my dad was a trooper. He was not going to let any urine-related obstacle get in the way of a good hockey game. We beat the Nordiques 5-2.

It would be an overstatement to say that lookage has haunted me in my adult years but it is still an issue. If you are reading this, you probably already know I'm not hung like a horse, but I am well-groomed and well-adjusted. I feel adequate enough to imagine some burly man admiring me at the trough. But this isn't exactly comforting. Still, when I revisited Winnipeg and its arena last year, I braved the old pissing trough for one last time, my eyes firmly locked on the lime green paint in front of me. The Winnipeg Arena will be demolished later this year. It was first erected in 1955 and expanded in 1979 to accommodate the NHL. And while I will miss the old barn, I can't help thinking that somewhere in St. Vital, there is one hockey dad who is taking the loss of the arena just a little harder than the rest of us.

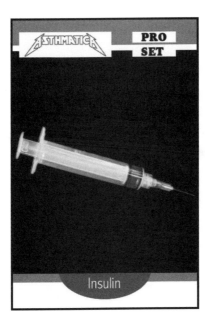

ASTHMATICA PRO SET

Insulin

Insulin Chic

Recently, at a Toronto literary hipster event, an older-generation writer approached me to call me out. If I am known at all for my writing, I am known for my using my own depression and various other afflictions as subject matter. The writer was angry at what he claimed was my flippancy and irresponsibility, and he accused me of glorifying the pill popping of my generation. "You know," he said, "in my day, we didn't have any of this 'depression' business. We just called it 'being sad' and we moved on!" To me this sounded a lot like: "You know, in my day, we didn't have any of this 'polio' business. We just called it 'flaccid paralysis' and we moved on!"

It's true that I have celebrated the use of antidepressants as medication. That's because antidepressants are medicinal in nature, and because they work. The pills alleviate many of the symptoms of depression such as apathy, irritability, hopelessness and the desire to write a novel about the history of Saskatchewan. To prove the efficacy of antidepressants I would have to do research, and research has shown that research is boring. However, I will offer that I would not be writing this right now had I not popped my trusty Effexor/Clonazepam combo about an hour ago. Instead I might be in bed, thinking of writing a letter to Lionel Richie about the recent problematic behaviour of his daughter.

When it comes to the celebration of illness and its treatment, I have even more potential. For instance, I am developing an aesthetic called "Insulin Chic," which is progressing at the same rate as my diabetes. As the modelling world celebrates "Heroin Chic" — the gaunt, anemic, skeletal body image — my aesthetic will trumpet the features of blurry vision, chronic urination and leg pain. Right now I have stage two diabetes — or, as my wife calls it, "laziness." I'm a little overweight but require no insulin shots or frequent doctor visits, and I can generally control my blood sugar by exercising and eating well. Since I can't think of a worse fate than having to exercise or eat well, I am well on my way to stage one, the money stage.

Stage one is where my aesthetic will really catch on. It often includes rapid weight loss, so although I will lose my eyesight, I will be a sight for sore eyes. One of my parents or a court-appointed custodian will help me get into my old size 28 jeans and what I assume is a very stylish button-down shirt, and I will swagger down the Main in my svelte new body with my trusty Seeing Eye dog, Sugar Twin, and my portable catheter, and people will swoon. Some jealous senior literary hipster will make a passing comment: "There goes Jonny. You know, in my day we just called it 'diabetes' but now they call it 'Insulin Chic.'"

ASTHMATICA

PRO SET

Inhalers

ASTHMATICA

Asthmatica is a realm of the rash-worthy and the professional bowler. Asthmatica is your nickname on the softball team. Asthmatica is wheeze-karaoke. Asthmatica is a penchant for knitting, and a hate on for dust mites. Asthmatica is a powder, a spray, a tonic, a choice. Asthmatica is a state that can only be achieved through daily meditation, rigourous self-reflexivity, and eight metered doses of salbutamol daily. Asthmatica is a place where you go when you need to wheeze alone. And you're happy there. Asthmatica is home.

THE LONGLIST

What the Moose Teach

Fulsome Evidence

Concerto in Hurt Minor

Talking to a Universe of Leaves

Three Kinds of Trees

Absence of Time's Absence

WolfWind

Making Strange to the Dark

Love's Leak

The Panther's Last Whimper

What Arrives at the Goodness

The Inevitability Conspiracy of the Night

When the Beans Spring Forth

The Density of Weight

What Happens when the Light Turns Dark

The Reflecting Mirror

A Picnic of Bees

A Painting of Glass and Water

On the Head of Mount Soleil

Grievous Epigraphs

The Amateur's Loom

These Hands, This Desire

Words without Symphonies

Making Love to the Ruins

The Tang of Sweet Nuts

A Winter Most Tender

The Mourning of Onions

Yarn Invaders!

ACKNOWLEDGEMENTS

I Wanna Be Your Alpha Male was published in *Headlight* and *Career Suicide!: Contemporary Literary Humour* (DC Books). *Insulin Chic* was published in *Geist*. *Hail, Satan* was published in *Prairie Fire*. *Previously Enjoyed Crosswords* was published in *Matrix*. *Rejected Essay Titles* and *The Longlist* were published in *Matrix* and co-written by David McGimpsey and Sarah Steinberg.

Thanks to Alana Wilcox, Jason McBride, Chandra Mayor, Sarah Steinberg, Alex Porco, Chris Charney, Angela Rawlings, Jason Camlot, Ryan Bigge, Andy Brown, Marc Ngui, Magda Wojtyra, Emily Schultz, Robert Allen, rob mclennan, Darcie Ferguson, Mark Walc and Daniel Varrette.

Thanks to my publisher, Mike O' Connor, for his continuing dedication to innovative literary publishing.

Thanks to my editor, Stephen Cain, for his hard work, keen eye and peculiar belief in me.

Thanks to David McGimpsey for his brilliant work and his friendship

Thanks to MC Palassio for her enthusiasm and patience.

Special thanks to Mom, Dad and Jamie for their support and understanding.

Special thanks to Tara and Lilly.

ABOUT THE AUTHOR

Jon Paul Fiorentino is a poet, editor and humorist. He lives in Montreal where he is the Managing Editor of *Matrix* magazine.

Also By The Author

Hello Serotonin (poems)
Resume Drowning (poems)
Transcona Fragments (poems)
Career Suicide!: Contemporary Literary Humour
(anthology)